I0424448

A Journey of Quotes to Building Your Dreams

A Journey of Quotes to Building Your Dreams

Antawn Barb & Joseph Barb III

Copyright © 2011 by Antawn Barb & Joseph Barb III.

Library of Congress Control Number:		2010918388
ISBN:	Hardcover	978-1-4568-3250-6
	Softcover	978-1-4568-3249-0
	Ebook	978-1-4568-3251-3

All rights reserved. No part of this book may be reproduced or transmitted in any form or by any means, electronic or mechanical, including photocopying, recording, or by any information storage and retrieval system, without permission in writing from the copyright owner.

This book was printed in the United States of America.

To order additional copies of this book, contact:
Xlibris Corporation
1-888-795-4274
www.Xlibris.com
Orders@Xlibris.com
89013

Antawn/Joseph would like to thank their family and friends for encouraging them to follow one of many dreams that they have been chasing for years. Only to hope inspire many others to follow their dreams while on that journey of life.

Thank you and enjoy reading A Journey of Quotes to Building Your Dreams!

Contents

Introduction

What makes a person not pursue the things he or she wants to do in life? Is it a lack money, lack of time. What makes a person not stop smoking, not loose the extra weight gained over the years? What about getting the job or even start that business adventure they always wanted?

What are the reasons or the excuses given? It's 100's or even thousands. The list could never end, if you don't end it. Well it can stop here! You can now be on control of your life for a change just by start reading a positive thought or thoughts regularly for at least 21 days straight. Building your Dreams with motivation Quotes is a great start for real change. Charles Swindol said, "10% is outside forces that we cannot control, but 90% is how we react to problem or situation."

This book is one of the many little golden nuggets that has come into your life while you are pursuing your goals and dreams.

Here are a collection of positive quotes and thoughts. Quotes by ordinary people like you and I to help you start on your new journey in life. Remember to find the joy you must go out on the journey. Only to find that the journey is the joy!

1

"read motivational quotes everyday, or better yet be motivated to create your own to inspire others to live life and live it well!" Antawn Barb w/antawn Joseph

2

"Do not wait; the time will never be 'just right.' Start where you stand, and work with whatever tools you may have at your command, and better tools will be found as you go along."

Napoleon Hill

There's never the right time', to get your goals started or your dreams realized. Just start now!! No one will do it for you.

3

"A person cannot directly choose his circumstances, but he can choose his thoughts, and so indirectly, yet surely, shape his circumstances."

James Allen

Choose to think thoughts that shape your destiny. Think success in your mind, and you will succeed in your goals and dreams.

4

"The secret to productive goal setting is in establishing clearly defined goals, writing them down and then focusing on them several times a day with words, pictures and emotions as if we've already achieved them."

Denis Waitley

It's important to set meaningful, and attainable goals. All that matters is you set some. Be determined to now to accomplish them.

5

Harriet Tubman says that, "Every great dream begins with a dreamer. Always remember, you have within you the strength, the patience, and the passion to reach for the stars to change the world."

You will change the world around you if you dream your dreams and place them in motion. Being a dreamer is a great start, but you must follow through.

"The only thing that stands between a man and what he wants from life is often merely the will to try it and the faith to believe that it is possible."

Richard M. DeVos

Only your actions will reveal what is truly your resolve. Will you have the will to go for your goal, your dream? Only you know! Only you!!

7

"Imagination is more important than knowledge. Knowledge is limited. Imagination encircles the world."

Albert Einstein(1879-1955)

Imagination is key. It begins in your mind with many thoughts and no limit to it.

"People with goals succeed because they know where they are going . . . It's as simple as that."

Earl Nightingale

Keep your goals simple and attainable. But, first you must write them down.

9

"Our attitudes control our lives. Attitudes are a secret power working 24 hours a day, for good or bad. It is of paramount importance that we know how to harness and control this great force."

Tom Blandi

What's your attitude that motivates you? Is it positive or negative?

10

Rockefeller once explained the secret of success. 'Get up early, work late—and strike oil.

I'm always grateful to get up early, but when I work late the rewards are well worth it. Think like Rockefeller and succeed!

11

"Keep away from people who try to belittle your ambitions. Small people always do that, but the really great make you feel that you, too, can become great."

Mark Twain

There are always people around who's not comfortable with what you do. By your actions you show them just what they should be doing. Continue forward with your goals, and share them only with the ones who will help you accomplish them.

12

"That which you think about, you create. Thoughts are things! And that which you think about, good or bad—you create into your reality."

Author Unknown

Continue to think success! Think success therefore, you create it.

13

The individual who know the score about life sees difficulties as opportunities.

Norman Vincent Peale

If you think not difficulties, but opportunities you conquer any task or challenge

14

Our greatest battles are that with our minds.

Jameson Frank

Control your mind, control your life

15

There are two ways of meeting difficulties: you alter the difficulties, or you alter yourself to meet them.

Phyllis Bottome

If you alter yourself, there are no difficulties, only opportunities to grow and start over again.

16

If you're bored with life—you don't get up every morning with a burning desire to do things—you don't have enough goals.

Lou Holtz

Set a lot of goals, and learn to have that burning desire to reach every goal.

Be a dreamer. If you don't know how to dream, you're dead.

Jim Valvano

Dreams are alive! So live through your dreams by getting in involved such as learning a new language, reading a new book monthly or even try running a marathon ☺ . Bring your dreams to a reality.

18

We should be dreaming. We grew up as kids having dreams, but now we're too sophisticated as adults, as a nation. We stopped dreaming. We should always have dreams.

Herb Brooks

Dreaming do not cost anything. It's actually fun, but even better when you pursue them and make them come true.

19

Do not wait for leaders; do it alone, person to person.

Mother Teresa

Sooner or later you must learn to stand alone, stand on your own and be the leader that's in you.

20

A man is but the product of his thoughts what he thinks, he becomes.

Mohandas Gandhi

Become what you think you should be. There are infinite opportunities to become what so desired. So first begin with your own thoughts.

21

"Success doesn't come to you, you go to it."

Marva Collins

Don't stand around, because it won't come. You must get into action and make things happen.

22

Success is a state of mind. If you want success, start thinking of yourself as a success.

Dr. Joyce Brothers

I'm success, you are success. Let's start believing it!

23

Nothing will work unless you do.

John Wooden

Work is the only way to becoming who you want be and what you want to accomplish in life. So work hard at whatever you do and success is sure to come.

24

The biggest adventure you can ever take is to live the life of your dreams.

Oprah Winfrey

The hardest thing for a person to do is to figure out what he or she wants. Once one figure it out, the adventure begins. The life of one's dream happens.

25

There are three ingredients in the good life: learning, earning and yearning.

Christopher Morley

And yet, one affects the other. Enjoy the good life! Get to know the main ingredients of your life.

26

Desire creates the power.

Raymond Holliwell

Cultivate the desire in order to continue on, then watch how the power will inspire you to accomplish great things.

27

Things turn out best for the people who make the best of the way things turn out.

John Wooden

Look at things in life as positive. Ask yourself, "What can I get from this experience?"

28

Forget the past—The future will give you plenty to worry about!

George Allen Sr.

Why waste energy on the past, especially the negative stuff. Learn from it and let's make a great start!

29

"It's better to hang out with people better than you. Pick out associates whose behavior is better than yours and you'll drift in that direction."

Warren Buffet

Mingle with positive people, who more positive than you and think thing upgrade.

30

Jim Rohn said, "Formal education will make you a living; self-education will make you a fortune."

It's not always about the money. It's about growing and learning from those little daily nuggets called life experiences.

31

"You have to learn the rules of the game. And then you have to play better than anyone else."

Albert Einstein

Just as an infant grows into adulthood, the key is who's teaching him the rules along the way in his life.

32

Make your enthusiasm about life contagious to others . . . .

Joseph Barb III

Influence others through your actions by being excited and enthused about everything!

33

Nourish the mind like you would the body. the mind can not survive on junk food.

Jim Rohn

What are you feeding your mind with? Read positive literature daily.

34

If you don't have enemies, you don't have character.

Paul Newman

Do you have character? Then you have enemies. Simply put, other people will not always agree with you. Really don't worry!

35

I don't know the key to success, but the key to failure is trying to please everybody.

Bill Cosby

The key to success lies within you and only you know what that is. Why waste time on what others think success should be for you.

36

Never bend your head. Hold it high. Look the world straight in the eye.

Helen Keller

Have good posture in your body and in your everyday life. You will encounter some difficulties as you live on, but remember, the greatest gift is life.

37

If you don't know where you are going, you will end up somewhere else.

Peter Lawrence

Just as a GPS (Global Positioning System) to get started, you must find out where you want to go. Type in your address and let the system guide you to your destination. Start dreaming and those dreams will guide you.

38

Usually when people are sad, they don't do anything. They just cry over their condition. But when they get angry, then they bring about change.

Malcolm X

It's up to you to get motivated to change to live a meaningful life whatever that is to you. Just do something that will bring joy and happiness to others and yourself.

39

Walk away from 97% of the people. Become part of the 3% that are doing things differently.

Jim Rohn

You're not like the 97% of the world. You are different simply because you choose to go on a "Journey of Dreams."

40

Nothing is stronger than a habit!

Ovid, Ars Amatoria

You will create many habits in a lifetime. Be sure the good replace those that are not so good. For example, like not getting enough rest or eating a balance meal etc.

41

There is always a way: if you are willing to commit.

Tony Robbins

The 'Way' is through your commitment. What are you committed to? How are you going to commit? When are you going to commit? Why should you commit? The answers lie within you, commit to something!

42

"No matter how old you are. The day you cannot sit down and come up with a want list, you are in trouble. You are on your way out."

Abraham Maslow

Sit down, make your want list! Don't delay, make a list today!

Conclusion

A *Journey of Quotes to Building Your Dreams* is the start of a great way for you, your family, friends and those whom you associate with to help further motivate yourself in theses challenging times.

We learn that motivation comes from all kinds of people, books, compact discs, movies, etc. But the real motivation is in you. Think about it. What if you were a light switch on the wall and no-one showed up to turn you on? You got to find a way to work. You got to want to achieve great things for yourself. Don't wait for someone to tell you "Ok it's your turn to lead." For some that day may never come! Motivate Yourself First, And then take the lead.

Encouragement is also needed. Back to the people you are around, the books you will read and movies you watch. Will these things encourage you to live the life desire? **You** have those answers to those dreams within.

So why do we look for ways to better ourselves? History shows that we strive for perfection. Better cars, better health, better way of living, right. Two words . . . . *We Care!* Just as those that helped us to this point in our life now, it is out of love that we want to succeed in whatever we wish to do. The quality to motivate, to encourage and love will cause all of us to live a journey happiness if they choose to.

A Journey of Quotes to Building Your Dreams would start you in creating more positive habits and thoughts and having new ideas by reading, journal writing, daily exercising and associating with great people.

Isn't that's what life is all about?

www.ingramcontent.com/pod-product-compliance
Lightning Source LLC
Chambersburg PA
CBHW050339290526
45785CB00006B/2562